Big Book Of Beginning Sounds

From Your Friends At The Mailbox® Magazine

Managing Editor:
Marie Iannetti

Concept Creator:
Cathy Whittle

Editors:
Debbie Blaylock
Lynn B. Coble

Illustrator:
Rebecca Saunders

Contributing Illustrators:
Jennifer Tipton Bennett
Pam Crane
Barry Slate

Cover art by:
Terri Anderson Lawson

Cover design by:
Jennifer Tipton Bennett

©1993 by THE EDUCATION CENTER, INC.
Reprinted 1994, 1996, 1997
All rights reserved except as here noted.

Table Of Contents

Dear Teacher,

Welcome to *The Big Book Of Beginning Sounds!* This all-time favorite book has been updated and revised to meet the changing needs of teachers. Revisions include all-new illustrations and awards, more nutritional cooking recipes, and the addition of several fun-filled learning centers and letter-sound-picture cards.

This book was developed to help you teach consonant letters and their sounds to youngsters. Featured on these pages are a variety of activities to involve, challenge, and delight your students as they learn the initial consonant sounds. Each letter in the book is presented in alphabetical order; you might choose to rearrange the activities so that your students can begin with the easiest sound and work their way up to the more difficult. We encourage you to augment, adapt, and supplement these materials to meet the needs of your students.

The many activities and review sheets provided will facilitate different teaching and learning styles. Guidelines and suggestions for use of these activities appear at the beginning of each section. The activities will provide stimulating hands-on experiences and allow children to discover and interact with the letters' sounds to promote internalization. It is our hope that you will find this book's activities to be valuable, positive learning experiences as your students discover the wonderful world of letters and their sounds!

The staff of The Education Center, Inc.

Cut And Place Worksheets

Each worksheet in this section features a large picture illustrating a beginning sound, with spaces left for the students to add cutouts of other words beginning with the same sound. Here are some ways to use these Cut And Place sheets:

— Duplicate a worksheet and cut-out page for each student. Provide scissors, paste, and crayons for a reinforcing art activity.

— Color and laminate each worksheet and its accompanying pieces. Cut out the pieces and place at a learning center. Have your students position the correct cutouts on the sheet. Color code the backs for self-checking, if desired.

Bb
butterfly

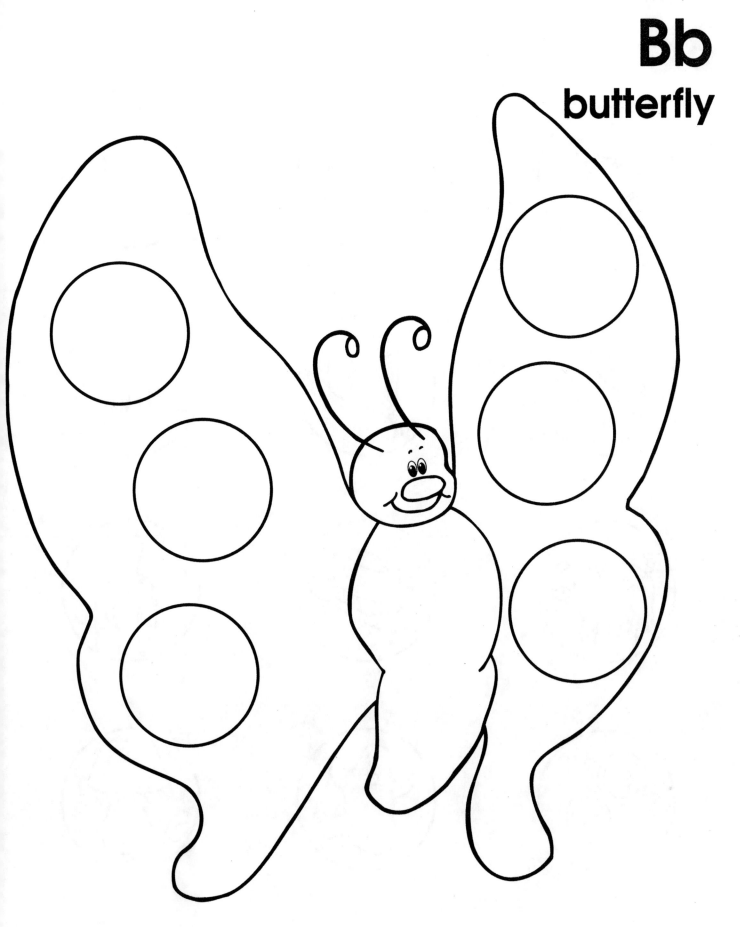

Bb

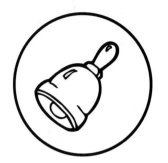  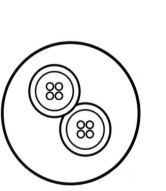

Cc
caterpillar

Cut and place

Dd
dog

Cut and place

Dd

 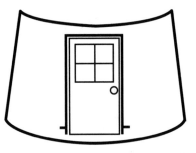 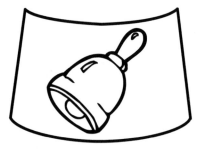

Ff
fish

Cut and place

Ff

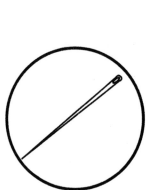  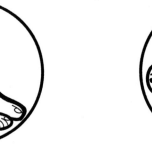

Gg
goose

Gg

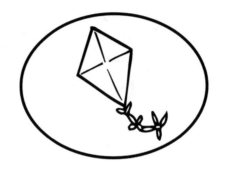

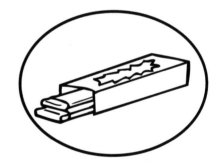

Hh
house

Cut and place

Hh

Jj
jars

Honey

Cut and place

Jj

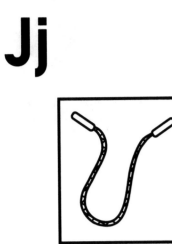  

Cut and place

Kk

kangaroo

Cut and place

Kk

 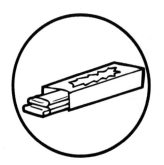 

Ll

lasso

25

Cut and place

Ll

Mm
monkey

Cut and place

Mm

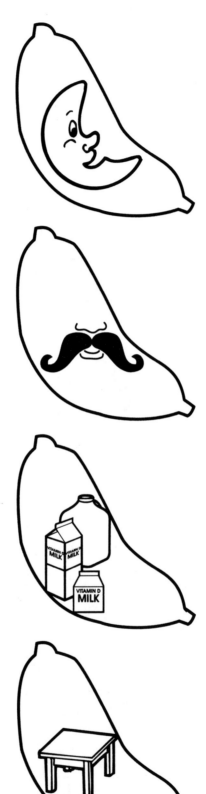
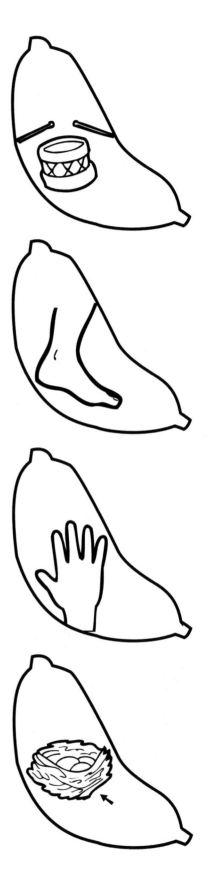

28

Nn
nest

Cut and place

Nn

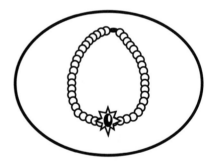

Pp
pig

Cut and place

Pp

Qq
quail

Cut and place

Rr
rabbit

Cut and place

Rr

 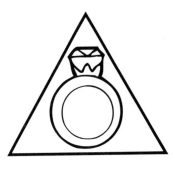 

Ss
seal

Cut and place

Ss

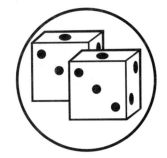

Tt
turtle

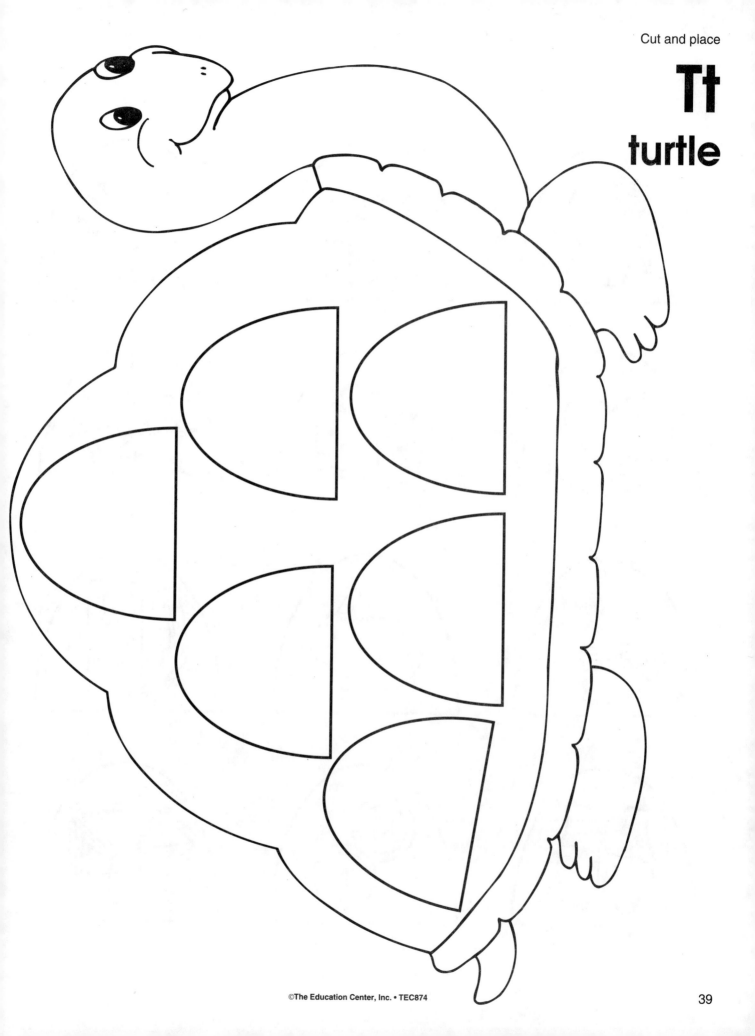

Cut and place

Tt

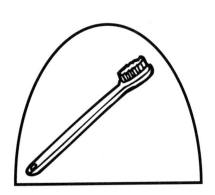  

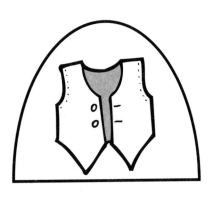 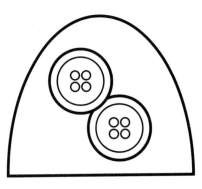 

Vv
vase

Cut and place

 Vv

Ww
web

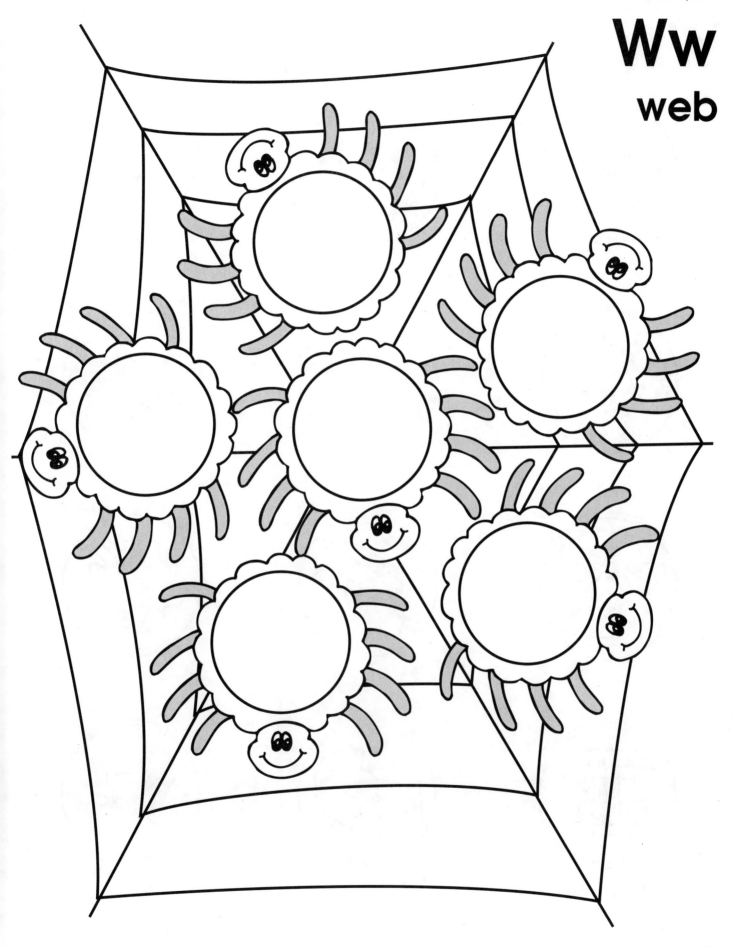

Cut and place

Ww

Yy
yarn

Zz
zebra

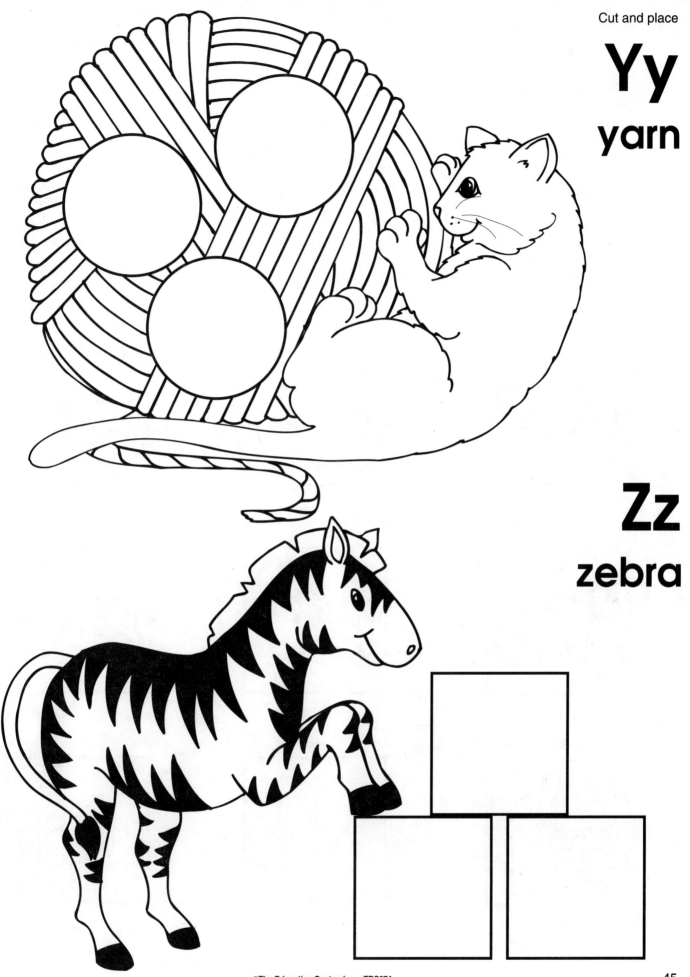

Cut and place

Yy Zz

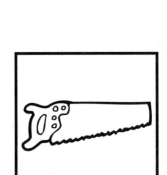

Review Cut And Place Worksheets

After teaching three letters individually, follow them up with a Review Cut And Place activity that groups the three together. As with the single-letter worksheets, students cut out pictures that begin with the indicated letters and place them in the correct spaces. Try these variations:

— Finished worksheets make a great bulletin board! Use an opaque projector to enlarge the central illustration for an eye-catching display on good work.

— Make an Open House booklet for parents to check their child's progress.

— Staple together blank Cut And Place sheets on three letters to make a student workbook. Duplicate an extra blank Review Cut And Place for the cover. As the student finishes the worksheet on one letter, he colors in the appropriate blanks on the cover, a signal to you that it's time to check his work.

— Cover a cardboard box with bright paper and make a slit in the top for students to deposit those cutouts they don't use in completing their worksheets. There are too many good uses for those pieces to let them get away—gameboards, playing cards, pin-on badges, learning centers, etc.

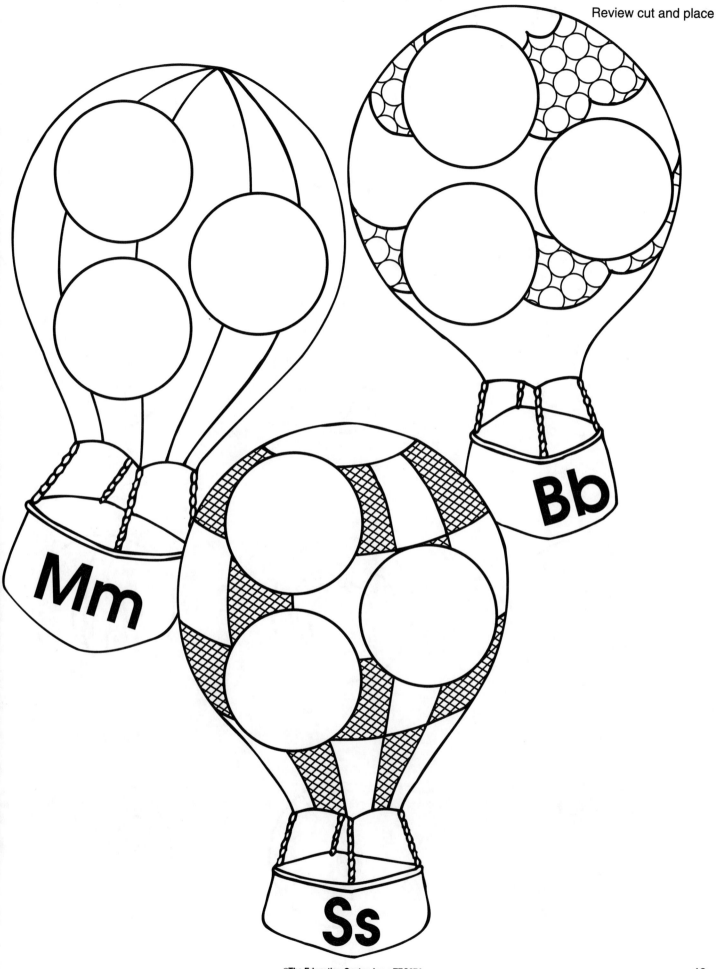

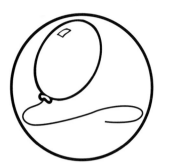

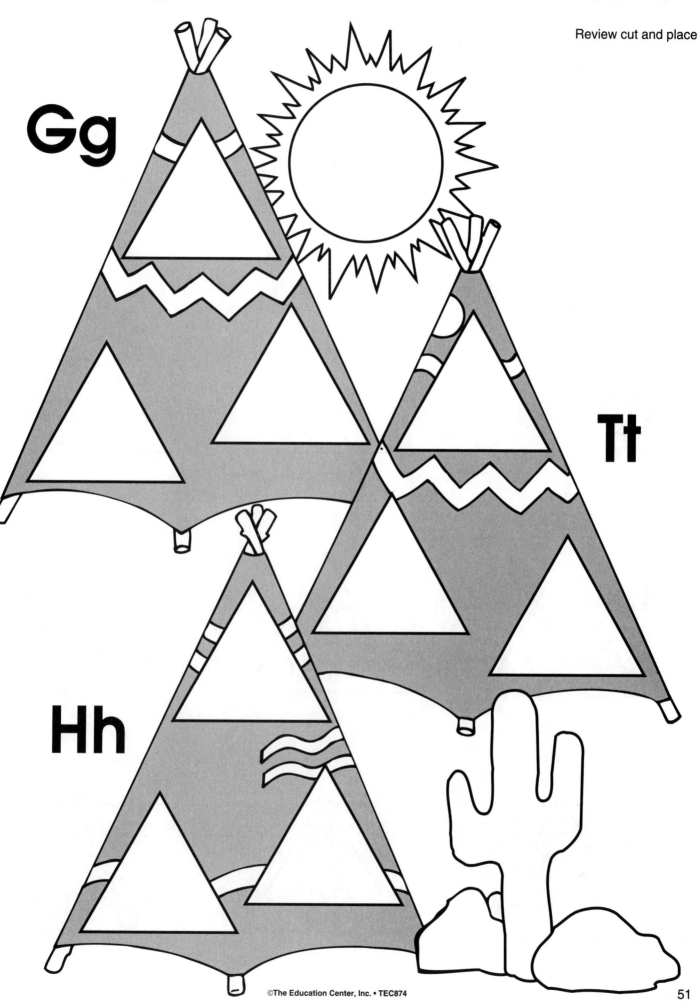

Gg

Tt

Hh

51

Review cut and place—G, H, T

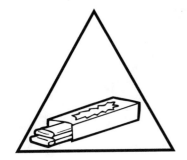  

Cc

Pp

Dd

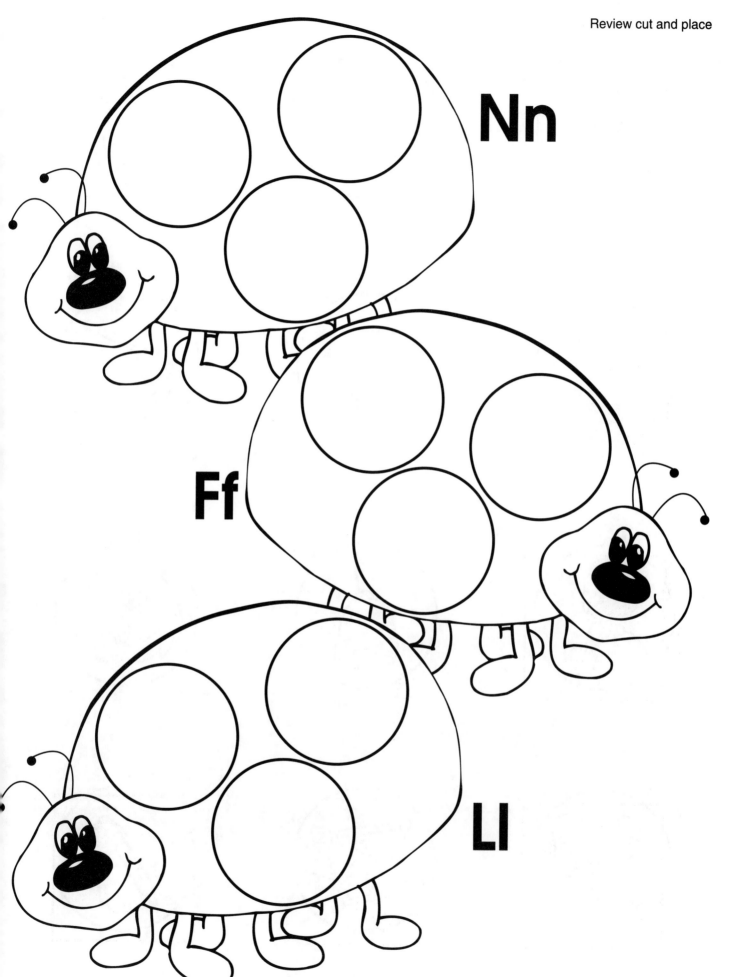

Nn

Ff

Ll

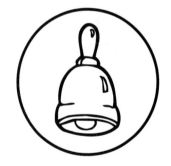

Qq   Zz

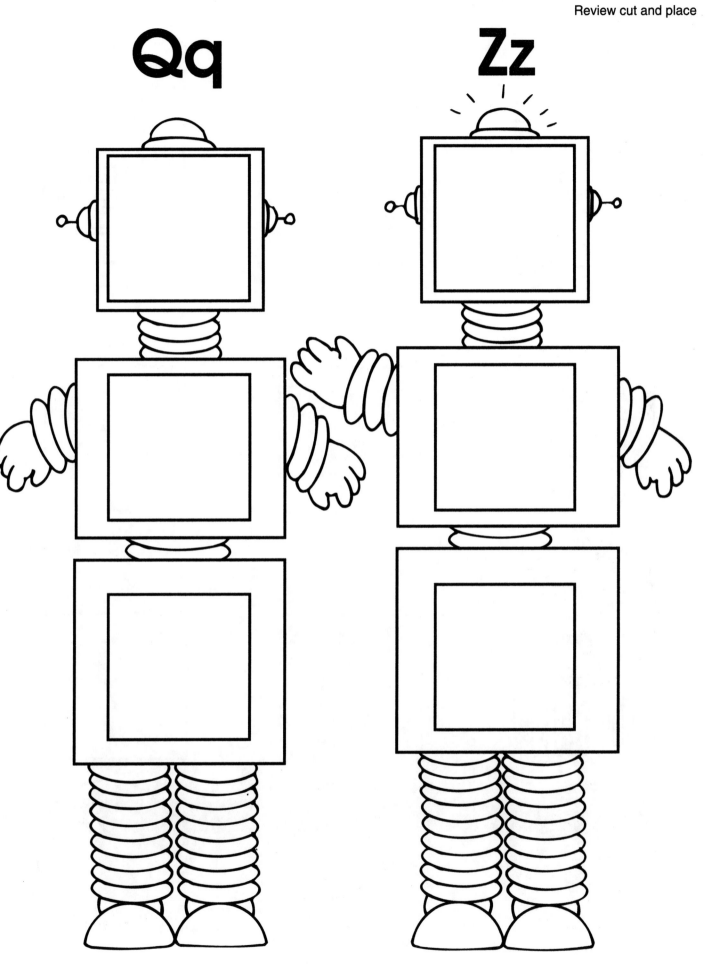

Jj

Vv

Rr

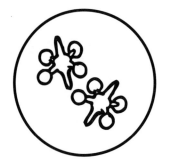

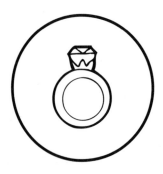

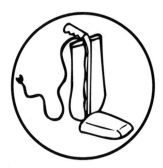

Ww

Kk

Yy

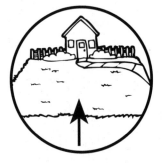

Lotto

Have students help in coloring these Lotto pages, and mount them on poster board for durability. Laminate if desired. Cut out all the playing circles and store with the boards in a box or large string-tie envelope. To play a review game on several letters, pull out one Lotto board for each student and place circles facedown on the table. In turn, each student chooses a circle and places it on his board if it matches. He returns the piece facedown to the pile if it does not match. The first student to fill his card is the winner. Follow these same playing rules for a Lotto game on a single sound, but duplicate several copies of each page and provide each student with the same card. Limit the variety of playing circles for the students to select from.

Bb
bear

Cc

castle

Dd

duck

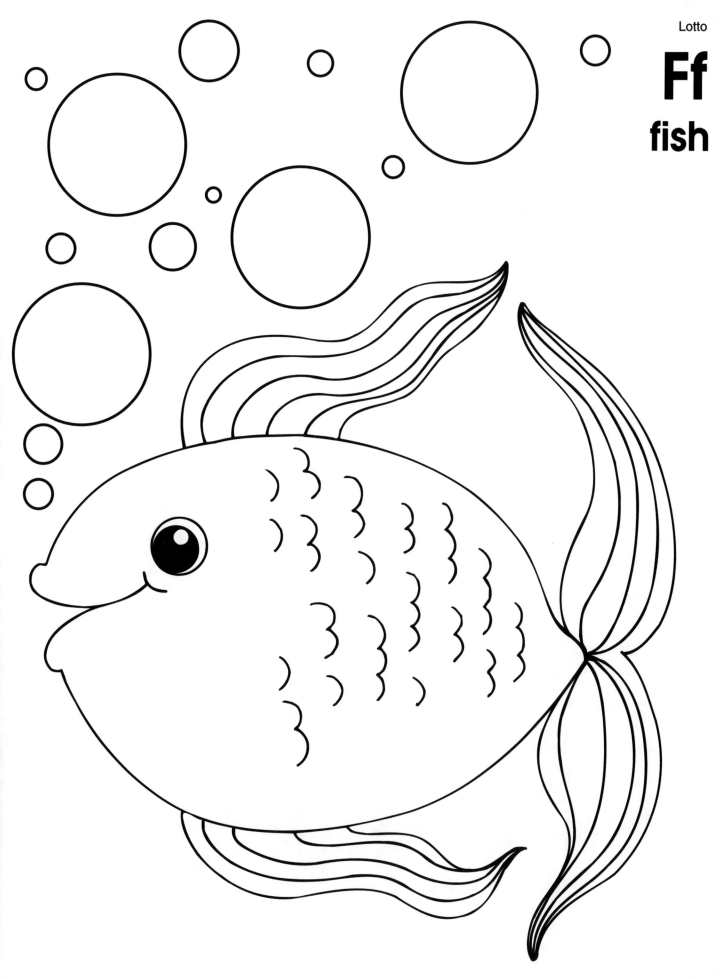

Gg

ghost

Hh
hippo

Jj

jack-in-the-box

Kk
kitten

Ll
ladybug

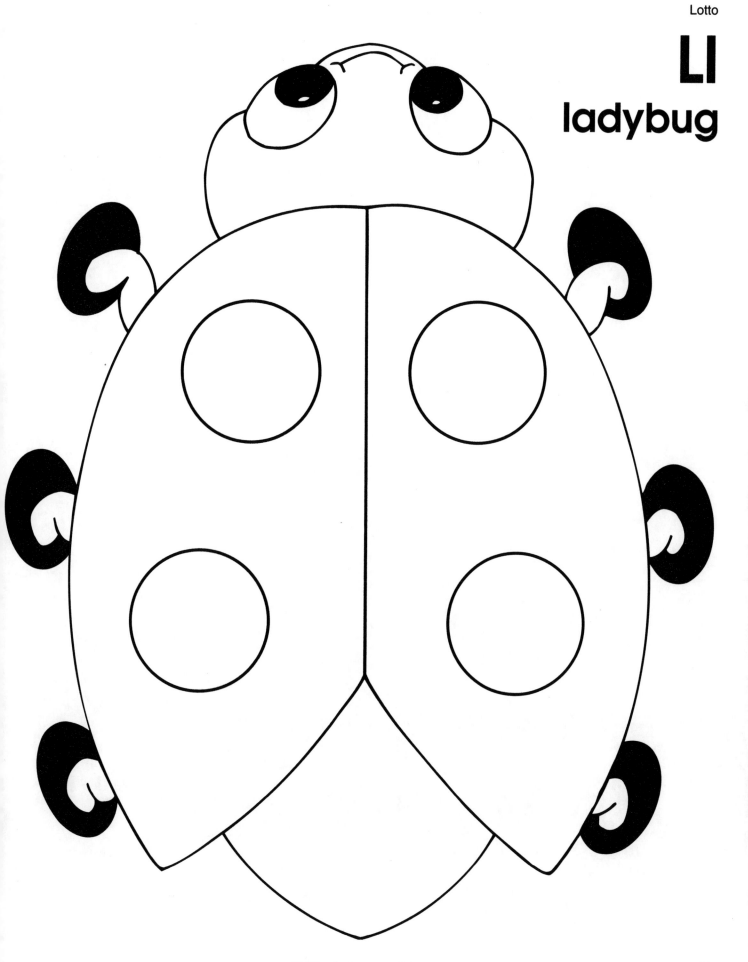

Mm
monkey

Nn
nuts

Pp
parrot

Qq
quilt

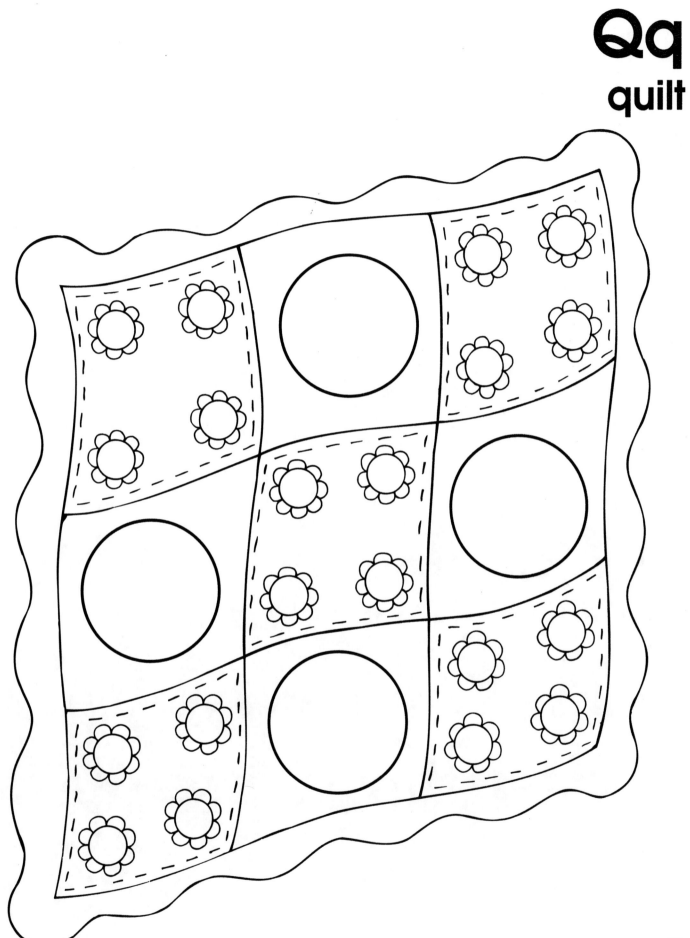

Rr
raccoon

Ss
sea horse

Tt
tiger

Vv
valentine

I Love You

Ww
walrus

Yy
yarn

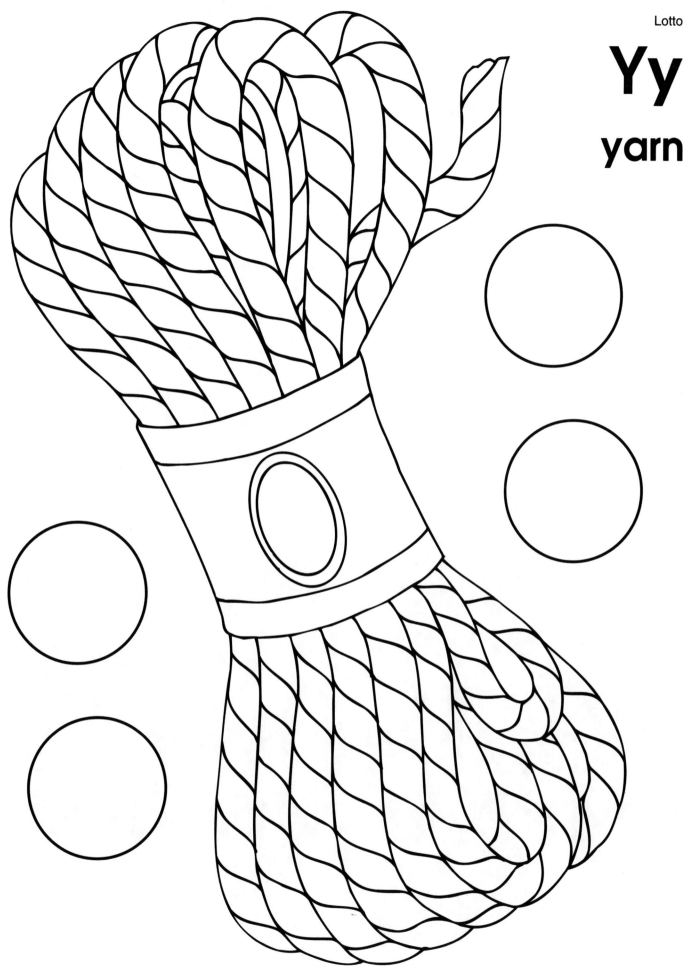

Zz
zipper

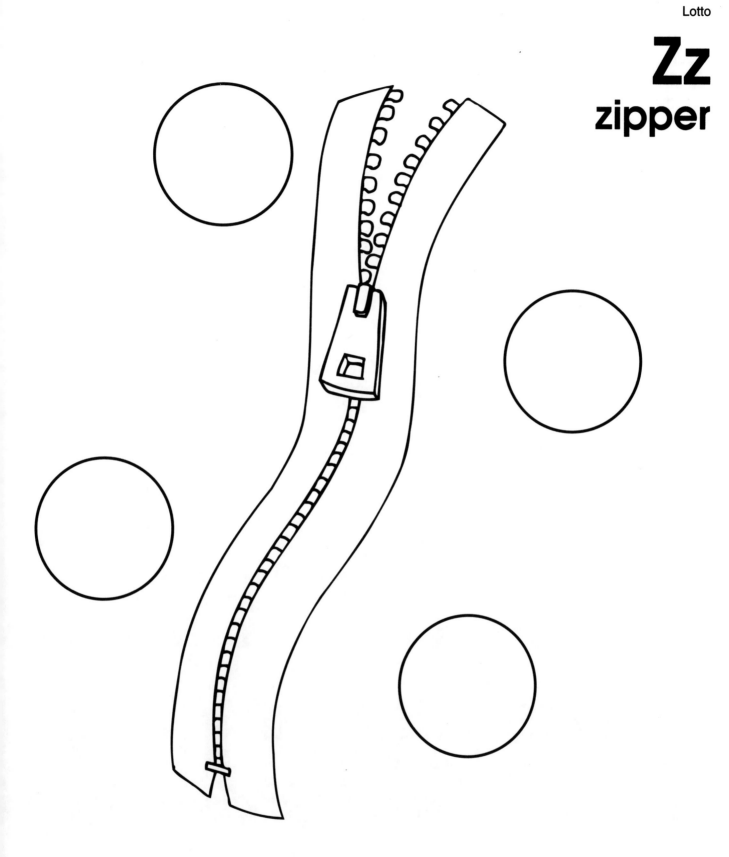

Bb Cc Dd Ff

Note To Teacher: Use with pages 65, 67, 69, and 71.

Gg   Hh   Jj   Kk

Note To Teacher: Use with pages 73, 75, 77, and 79.

Ll   Mm   Nn   Pp

Note To Teacher: Use with pages 81, 83, 85, and 87.

Qq Rr Ss Tt

Note To Teacher: Use with pages 89, 91, 93, and 95.

Vv   Ww   Yy   Zz

Note To Teacher: Use with pages 97, 99, 101, and 103.

Recipes

What better way to stir up excitement and learn about letter sounds than with fun cooking experiences! Use these nifty recipes to introduce each initial consonant sound or to applaud its mastery by your students. Encourage your little chefs to help measure, stir, pour, mix, read the recipes, and, of course, eat and enjoy the finished products. How about having your students plan and organize a Beginning Sound Banquet at the end of the year? Involving parents to assist and asking them to donate ingredients will help defray the expenses. Duplicate the recipes and make a cookbook for each child to take home to share with his parents—a learning experience for all!

Recipe For Learning

Take curious youngsters and fold in 1 cup of wonder. Blend well, until the youngsters are ready to explore. Stir in a pinch of imagination. Add a handful of experience and creativity. Blend in a dash of enthusiasm. Serve with 2 tablespoons of interest and sprinkle with fun!

Serving size: 1 classroom

Bb

Baked Bananas

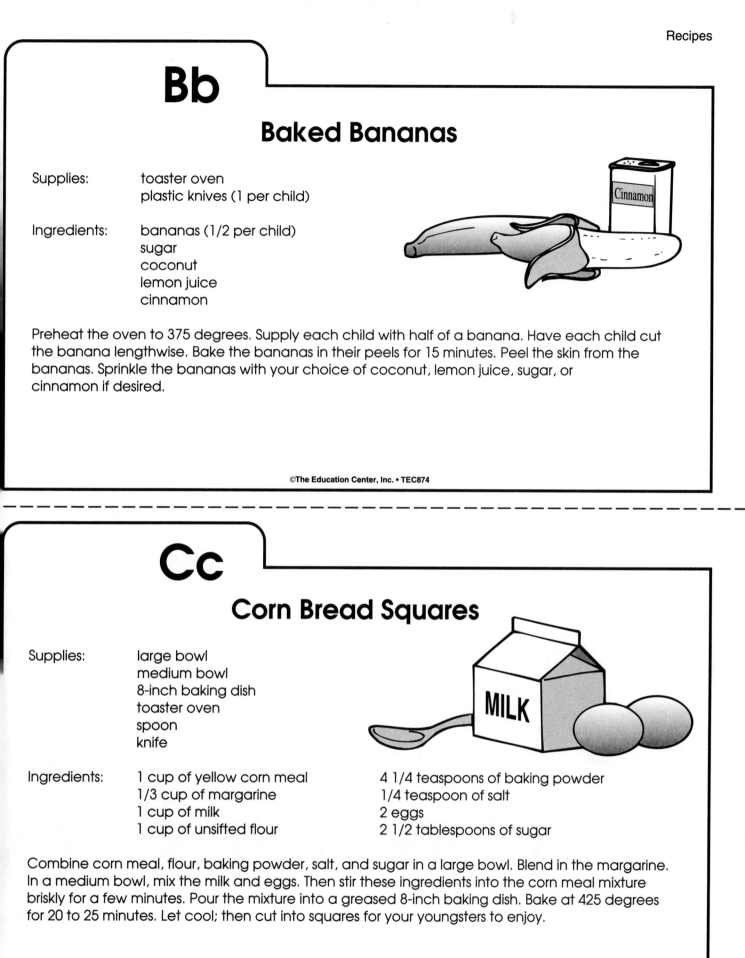

Supplies: toaster oven
             plastic knives (1 per child)

Ingredients: bananas (1/2 per child)
             sugar
             coconut
             lemon juice
             cinnamon

Preheat the oven to 375 degrees. Supply each child with half of a banana. Have each child cut the banana lengthwise. Bake the bananas in their peels for 15 minutes. Peel the skin from the bananas. Sprinkle the bananas with your choice of coconut, lemon juice, sugar, or cinnamon if desired.

©The Education Center, Inc. • TEC874

Cc

Corn Bread Squares

Supplies: large bowl
             medium bowl
             8-inch baking dish
             toaster oven
             spoon
             knife

Ingredients: 1 cup of yellow corn meal   4 1/4 teaspoons of baking powder
             1/3 cup of margarine   1/4 teaspoon of salt
             1 cup of milk   2 eggs
             1 cup of unsifted flour   2 1/2 tablespoons of sugar

Combine corn meal, flour, baking powder, salt, and sugar in a large bowl. Blend in the margarine. In a medium bowl, mix the milk and eggs. Then stir these ingredients into the corn meal mixture briskly for a few minutes. Pour the mixture into a greased 8-inch baking dish. Bake at 425 degrees for 20 to 25 minutes. Let cool; then cut into squares for your youngsters to enjoy.

©The Education Center, Inc. • TEC874

Dd

Dandy Dip

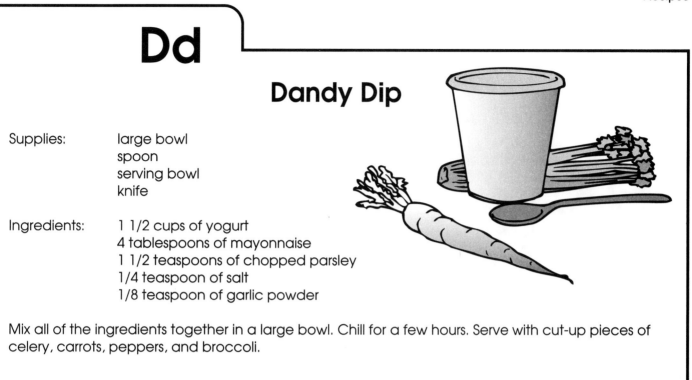

Supplies: large bowl
             spoon
             serving bowl
             knife

Ingredients: 1 1/2 cups of yogurt
                4 tablespoons of mayonnaise
                1 1/2 teaspoons of chopped parsley
                1/4 teaspoon of salt
                1/8 teaspoon of garlic powder

Mix all of the ingredients together in a large bowl. Chill for a few hours. Serve with cut-up pieces of celery, carrots, peppers, and broccoli.

Ff

Funny Fruity Faces

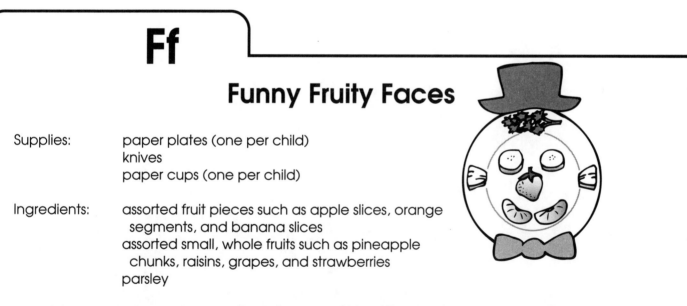

Supplies: paper plates (one per child)
             knives
             paper cups (one per child)

Ingredients: assorted fruit pieces such as apple slices, orange
                  segments, and banana slices
                assorted small, whole fruits such as pineapple
                  chunks, raisins, grapes, and strawberries
                parsley

Provide each youngster with a cup full of assorted fruit, a piece of parsley, and a paper plate. Have your students arrange the fruit on the plate to make funny fruity faces and the parsley leaves to represent hair. Have your youngsters add construction-paper hats and accessories to their fruity faces.

Gg

Goody-Goody Granola

Supplies: large bowl
electric skillet
spoon

Ingredients: 4 cups of rolled oats
1 1/4 cups of wheat germ
1 cup of honey
1 cup of oil
3/4 cup of chopped nuts
2 1/2 teaspoons of cinnamon
1/4 teaspoon of nutmeg
1/2 cup of raisins
1/2 cup of sesame seeds

Mix the first seven ingredients together in a large bowl. Cook the mixture in an electric skillet at 325 degrees for 10 minutes or until browned, stirring often. Let the mixture cool; then mix in the raisins and sesame seeds, and serve.

Hh

Honey Cookies

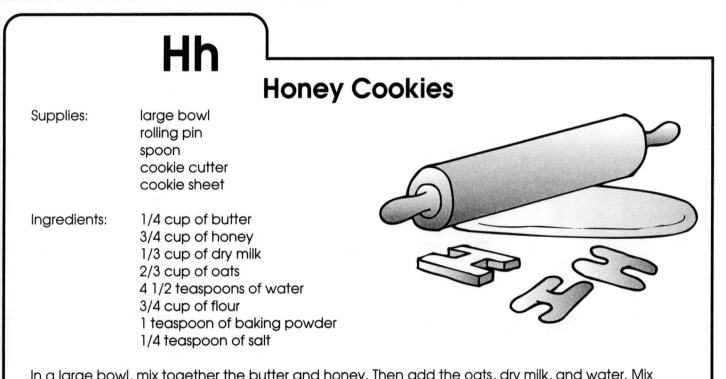

Supplies: large bowl
rolling pin
spoon
cookie cutter
cookie sheet

Ingredients: 1/4 cup of butter
3/4 cup of honey
1/3 cup of dry milk
2/3 cup of oats
4 1/2 teaspoons of water
3/4 cup of flour
1 teaspoon of baking powder
1/4 teaspoon of salt

In a large bowl, mix together the butter and honey. Then add the oats, dry milk, and water. Mix well. Blend in the flour, baking powder, and salt. Roll out dough to 1/4" thick. Cut the dough with your favorite cookie cutter (maybe an "H"-shaped cutter). Bake at 325 degrees for 10 to 12 minutes. Sprinkle with powdered sugar if desired. Makes approximately 12 cookies. Yum!

Jj

Jumble Juice Popsicles

Supplies: paper cups (one per child)
             plastic teaspoons (one per child)
             freezer
             large container

Ingredients: 24 ounces of grape juice
                24 ounces of apple juice

Mix the two juices together in a large container. Pour the juice into the paper cups. Insert a spoon into each cup, with the handles facing up. Freeze.

Kk

Kicky Cooler Kabobs

Supplies: skewers (one per child)
             paper plates
             oblong bowl
             plastic kniives

Ingredients: banana chunks
                apple chunks
                melon chunks
                pear chunks
                marshmallows
                orange juice
                shredded coconut

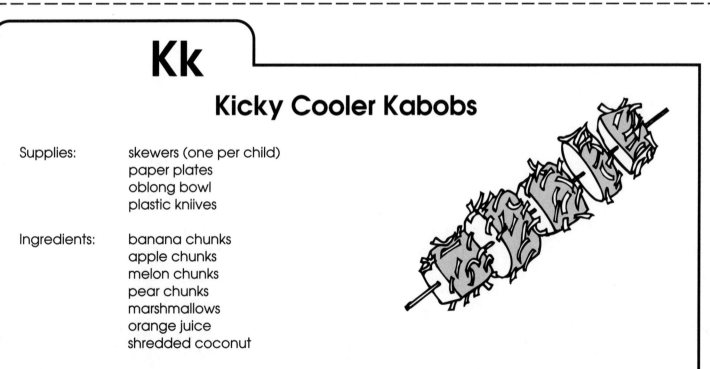

Have the youngsters help cut the various fruits and place them in individual paper plates. Pour the orange juice in an oblong bowl. Place the paper plates and the bowl on a table. Provide each youngster with a wooden skewer and have him create his own kabob. Have each child dip his kabob in the orange juice, then roll it in the shredded coconut.

Ll

Lemonade

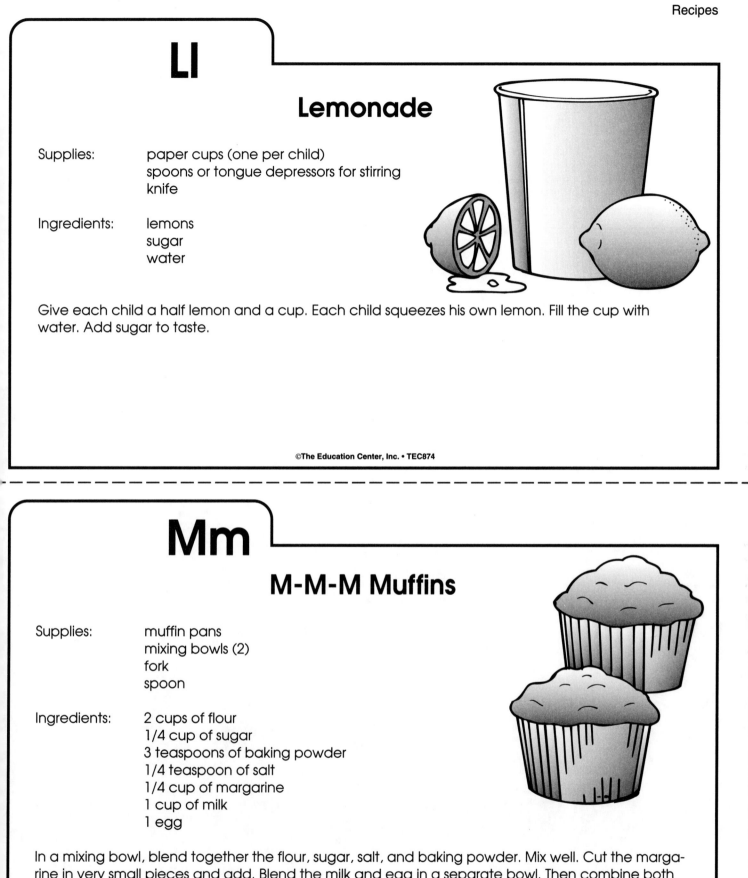

Supplies: paper cups (one per child)
            spoons or tongue depressors for stirring
            knife

Ingredients: lemons
               sugar
               water

Give each child a half lemon and a cup. Each child squeezes his own lemon. Fill the cup with water. Add sugar to taste.

Mm

M-M-M Muffins

Supplies: muffin pans
            mixing bowls (2)
            fork
            spoon

Ingredients: 2 cups of flour
               1/4 cup of sugar
               3 teaspoons of baking powder
               1/4 teaspoon of salt
               1/4 cup of margarine
               1 cup of milk
               1 egg

In a mixing bowl, blend together the flour, sugar, salt, and baking powder. Mix well. Cut the margarine in very small pieces and add. Blend the milk and egg in a separate bowl. Then combine both mixtures together. Stir briskly with a fork until all of the dry ingredients are moist. Pour the batter evenly in a greased muffin pan. Bake at 400 degrees for 20 to 25 minutes. Makes 12 muffins.

Nn

Nifty Nachos

Supplies: cookie sheet
                   teaspoon

Ingredients: nacho chips
                   assorted shredded cheeses
                   chopped black olives
                   1 pint of sour cream
                   optional: chopped green chilies

Give each child several nacho chips. Have each of your youngsters place his chips on a cookie sheet. Sprinkle with shredded cheese. Bake at 350 degrees until the cheese melts. Let cool. Serve with a teaspoon of sour cream. Top with olives. Some of your adventurous students may wish to try a tiny piece of green chili on their nachos.

Pp

Pizza

Supplies: toaster oven
                   knives

Ingredients: pizza sauce
                   mozzarella cheese
                   canned biscuits (one per child)

Give each child a canned biscuit and have him press it flat. Top it with pizza sauce and cheese. Bake in the toaster oven at 425 degrees until the biscuit is done.

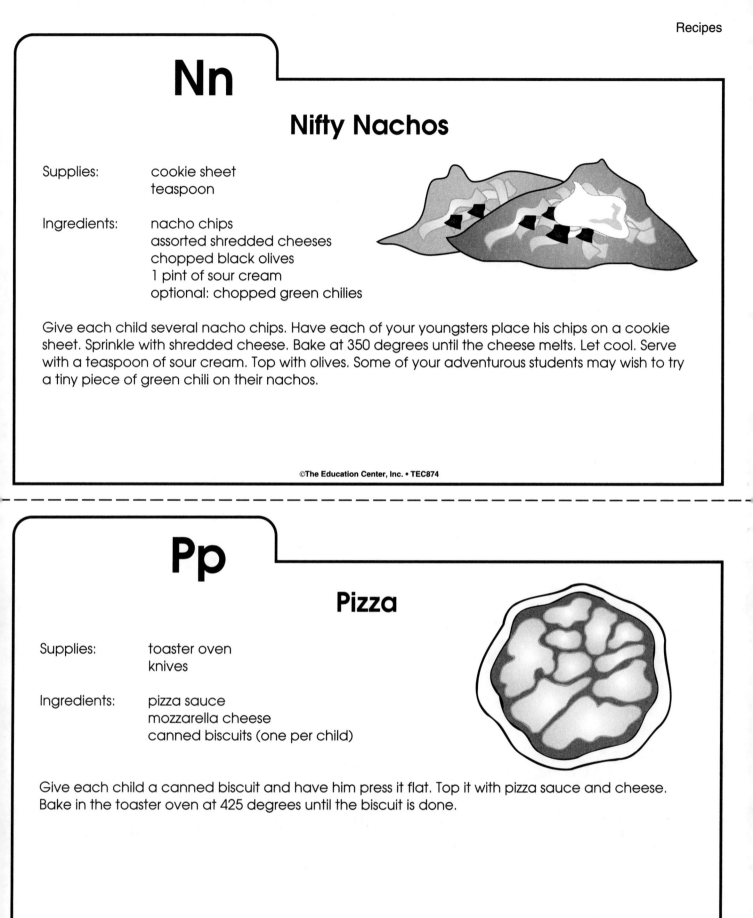

Qq
Quaker Oatmeal Cookies

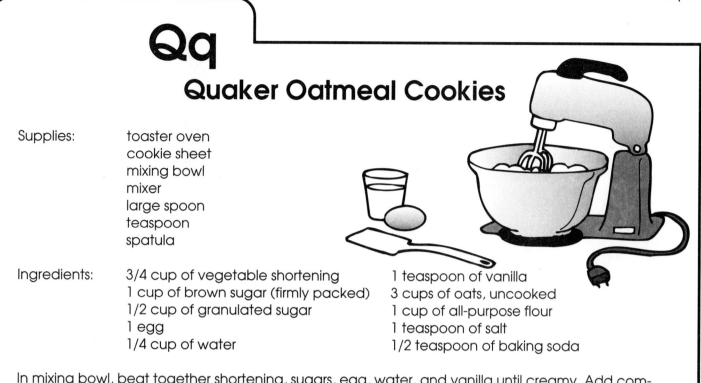

Supplies:
toaster oven
cookie sheet
mixing bowl
mixer
large spoon
teaspoon
spatula

Ingredients:
3/4 cup of vegetable shortening
1 cup of brown sugar (firmly packed)
1/2 cup of granulated sugar
1 egg
1/4 cup of water

1 teaspoon of vanilla
3 cups of oats, uncooked
1 cup of all-purpose flour
1 teaspoon of salt
1/2 teaspoon of baking soda

In mixing bowl, beat together shortening, sugars, egg, water, and vanilla until creamy. Add combined remaining ingredients; mix well. Drop rounded teaspoonfuls on greased cookie sheet. Bake in preheated moderate oven (350 degrees) 12 to 15 minutes. Makes about five dozen cookies.

Rr
Rice Pudding

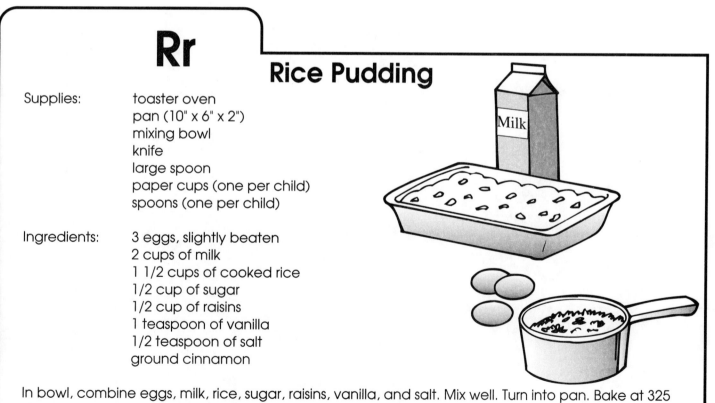

Supplies:
toaster oven
pan (10" x 6" x 2")
mixing bowl
knife
large spoon
paper cups (one per child)
spoons (one per child)

Ingredients:
3 eggs, slightly beaten
2 cups of milk
1 1/2 cups of cooked rice
1/2 cup of sugar
1/2 cup of raisins
1 teaspoon of vanilla
1/2 teaspoon of salt
ground cinnamon

In bowl, combine eggs, milk, rice, sugar, raisins, vanilla, and salt. Mix well. Turn into pan. Bake at 325 degrees for 25 minutes. Stir; sprinkle with cinnamon. Continue baking 20 to 25 minutes longer, until knife inserted in the center comes out clean. Serve in paper cups.

Ss

S'mores

Supplies: toaster oven
             spatula

Ingredients: large marshmallows
                Hershey chocolate bars
                graham crackers

Using two graham cracker squares, a piece of chocolate bar,
and one large marshmallow, each child makes a sandwich. Bake in
the toaster oven until the marshmallows melt.

Tt

Tea And Toast

Supplies: hot plate
             pitcher
             saucepan
             spoon
             cups (one per child)
             toaster oven
             knife

Ingredients: tea bags
                sugar
                milk (optional)
                butter
                bread
                jam

Prepare hot tea according to the directions on the package. Add sugar. Some of your students
may wish to add milk. Toast bread in the toaster oven. Serve with butter and jam.

Vv

Vegetable Soup

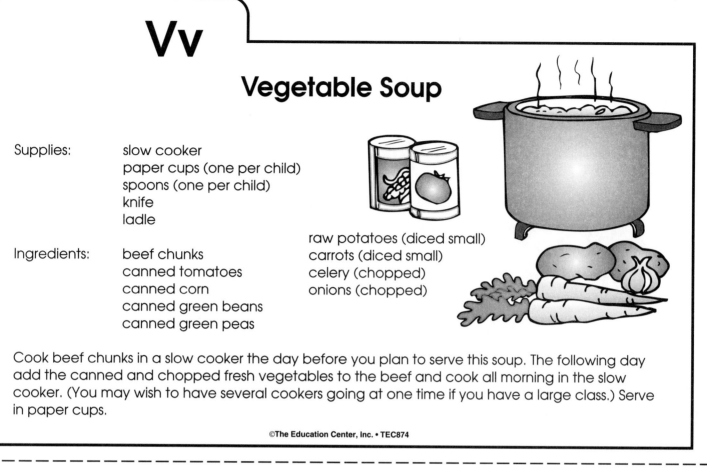

Supplies: slow cooker
             paper cups (one per child)
             spoons (one per child)
             knife
             ladle

Ingredients: beef chunks
                canned tomatoes
                canned corn
                canned green beans
                canned green peas

raw potatoes (diced small)
carrots (diced small)
celery (chopped)
onions (chopped)

Cook beef chunks in a slow cooker the day before you plan to serve this soup. The following day add the canned and chopped fresh vegetables to the beef and cook all morning in the slow cooker. (You may wish to have several cookers going at one time if you have a large class.) Serve in paper cups.

©The Education Center, Inc. • TEC874

Ww

Waffles

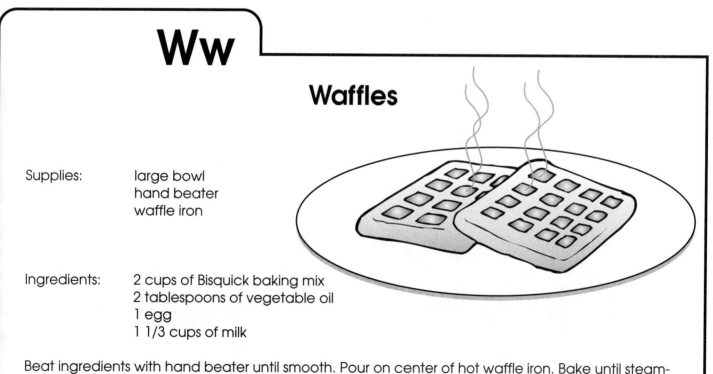

Supplies: large bowl
             hand beater
             waffle iron

Ingredients: 2 cups of Bisquick baking mix
                2 tablespoons of vegetable oil
                1 egg
                1 1/3 cups of milk

Beat ingredients with hand beater until smooth. Pour on center of hot waffle iron. Bake until steaming stops. Remove carefully. Makes three 9-inch waffles. Option: Prepare frozen waffles in a toaster instead of making them from scratch.

©The Education Center, Inc. • TEC874

Yy

Yum-Yum Yogurt

Supplies:
spoons (one per child)
fork (one per child)
small plastic bowls (one per child)
paper plates
4 tablespoons

Ingredients:
1/2 cup of plain yogurt (per child)
banana chunks
blueberries
sliced strawberries
peach chunks
1 teaspoon of powdered milk (per child)

Place the fruit in separate paper plates. Put all of the plates of fruit on a table. Supply each child with a small plastic bowl. Have each child take 3 tablespoons of the fruit of his choice and place it in the bowl. Have each youngster mash his fruit with a fork. Add the yogurt and the powdered milk to each child's bowl. Have your youngsters mix the yogurt well before eating.

Zz

Zippy Zucchini Bread

Supplies:
large bowl
loaf pans (2)
spoon

Ingredients:
2 2/3 cups of raw grated zucchini
3 eggs
1 cup of oil
2 cups of packed brown sugar
3 cups of flour
1 cup of raisins
1 cup of chopped nuts
1 teaspoon of baking soda
1 tablespoon of vanilla extract
1 teaspoon of salt

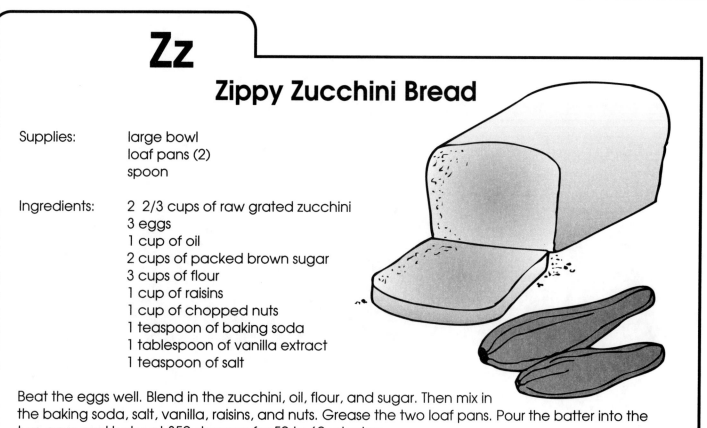

Beat the eggs well. Blend in the zucchini, oil, flour, and sugar. Then mix in the baking soda, salt, vanilla, raisins, and nuts. Grease the two loaf pans. Pour the batter into the two pans and bake at 350 degrees for 50 to 60 minutes.

Sound Bracelets

Your students will love making and wearing their very own Sound Bracelets. Duplicate the Sound Bracelets on construction paper and fasten with tape. For a permanent classroom set of bracelets, mount them on laminated poster board or lightweight vinyl wallpaper colored with permanent markers. Use the bracelets as an award for a letter that proves especially difficult or distribute them to the whole class as an introduction to a sound. Or have a Dress-Up Day: ask each child to wear an item of clothing that begins with the letter on his Sound Bracelet.

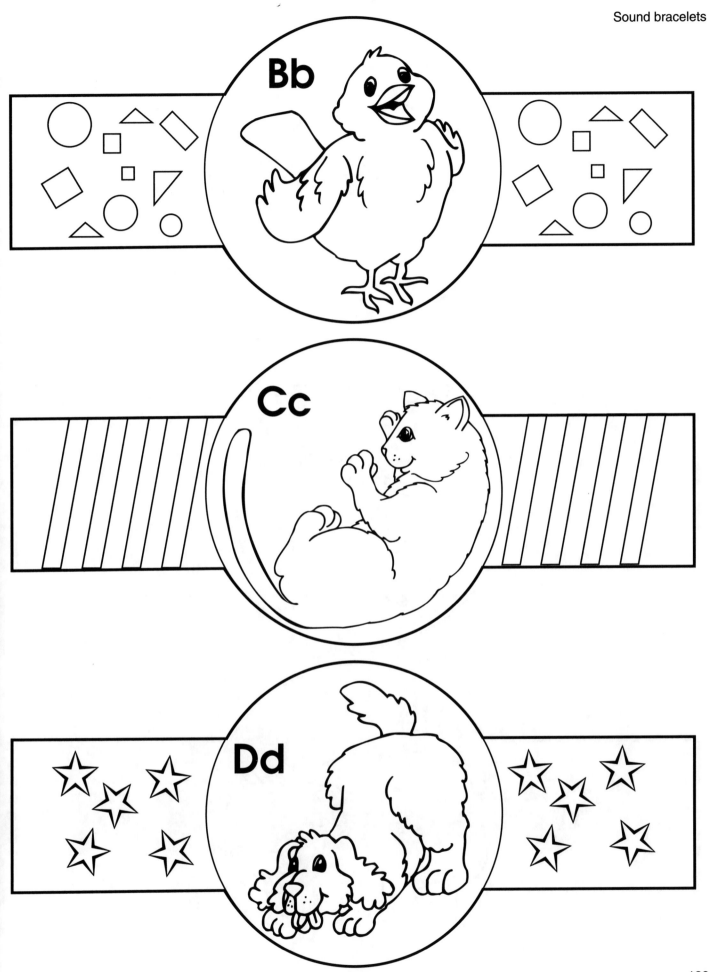

Jj

Kk

Ll

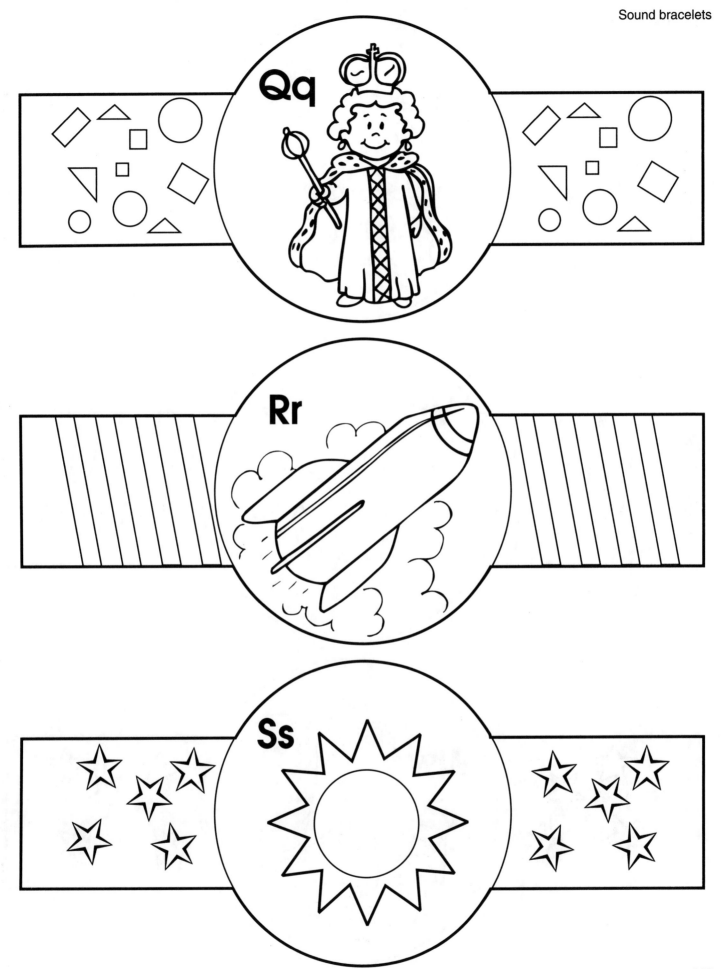

Qq

Rr

Ss

Sound bracelets

©The Education Center, Inc. • TEC874

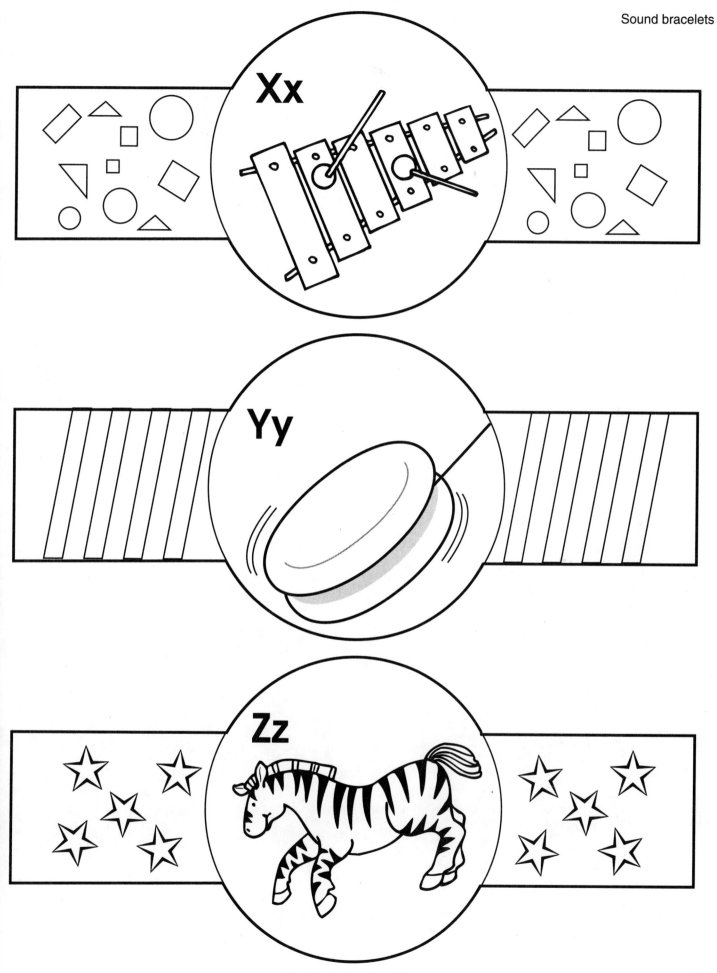

Learning Centers

This section features five learning centers and picture cards to use to reinforce and review initial consonant sounds. We suggest that you color each center and cut it out along the black line surrounding the center. Glue the two sections of each center together. Mount the center on poster board; then laminate if desired. Each center can be used for a bulletin board; can be placed on the blackboard, the door, or the floor; can be placed at a table; or can be used as a teaching aid when you are working with a small group. Plan to make your centers reusable. Change the center pieces or skills when desired. Your youngsters are sure to enjoy these nifty hands-on learning centers!

Match each picture on page 151 to its matching initial consonant. Code the backs of the center pieces for self-checking if desired.

Pick Of

Dd

Jj

Kk

Ff

The Crop!

Match each picture on page 155 to its matching initial consonant. Code the backs of the center pieces for self-checking if desired.

Hot-Diggity

Mm

Qq

©The Education Center, Inc. • TEC874

Dogs!

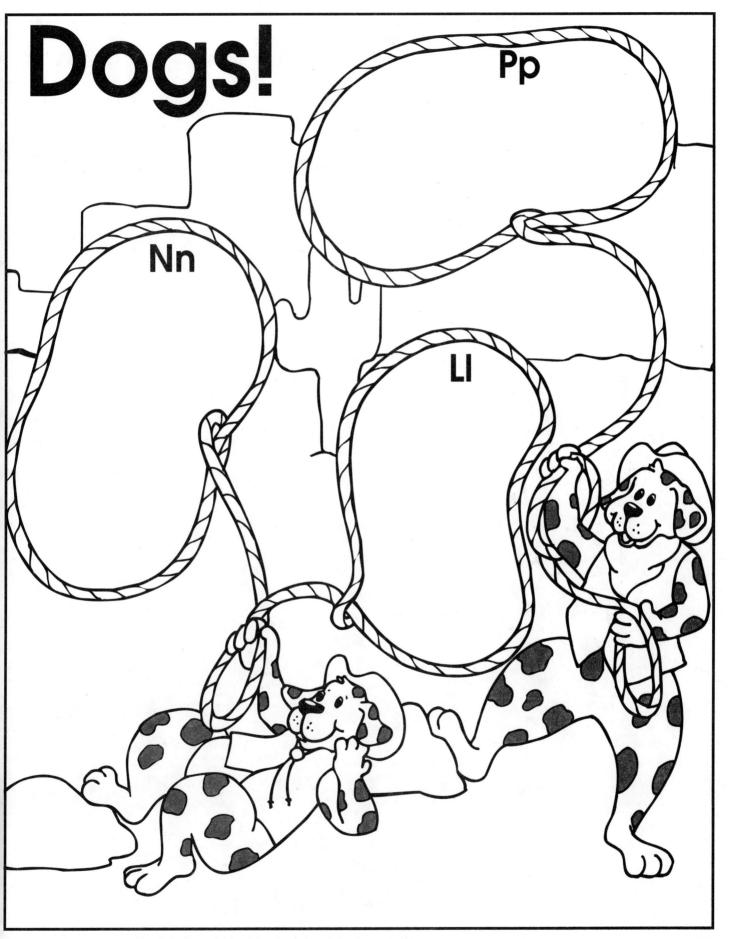

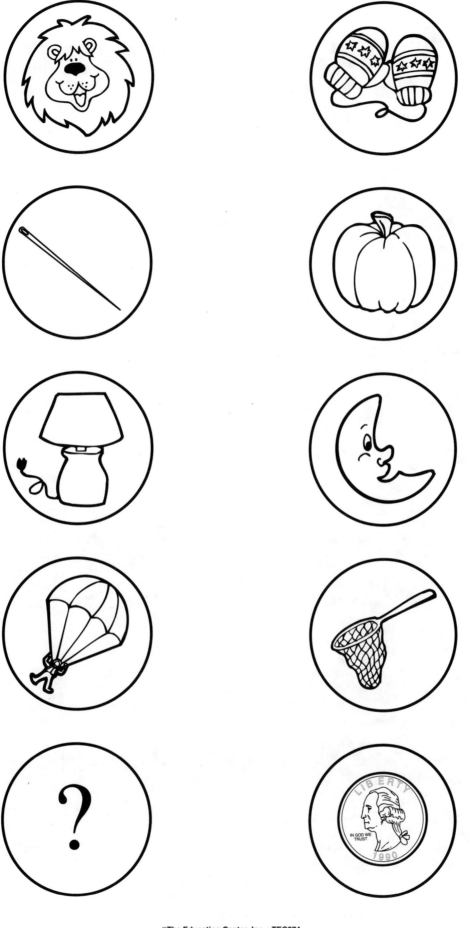

See page 159 for the pieces. Provide game markers.

More Cheese

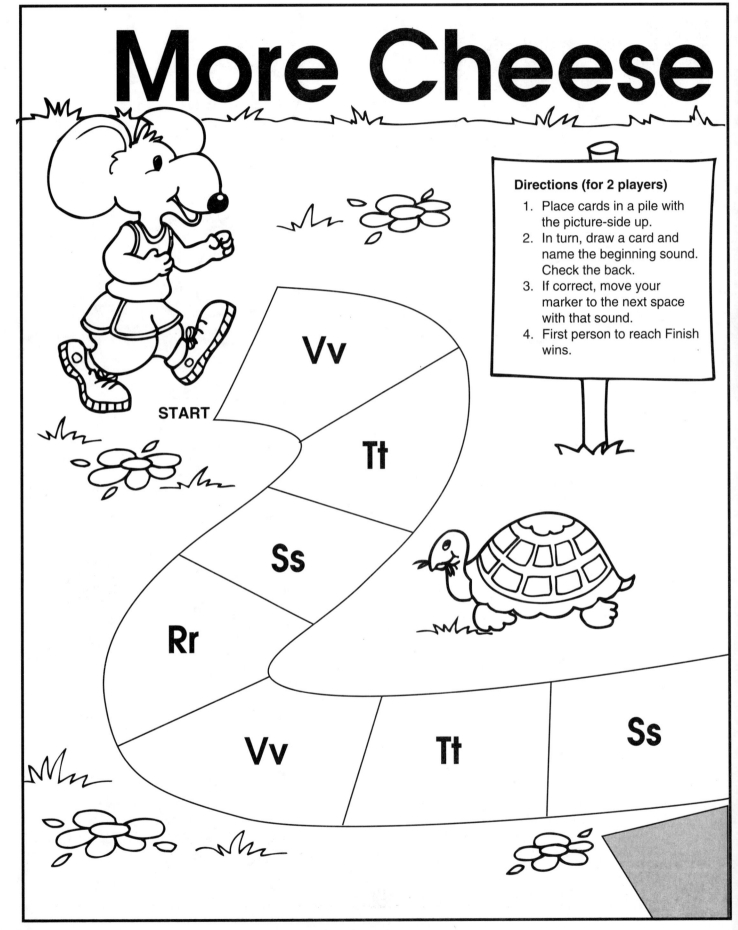

Directions (for 2 players)

1. Place cards in a pile with the picture-side up.
2. In turn, draw a card and name the beginning sound. Check the back.
3. If correct, move your marker to the next space with that sound.
4. First person to reach Finish wins.

START

Vv

Tt

Ss

Rr

Vv

Tt

Ss

Please!

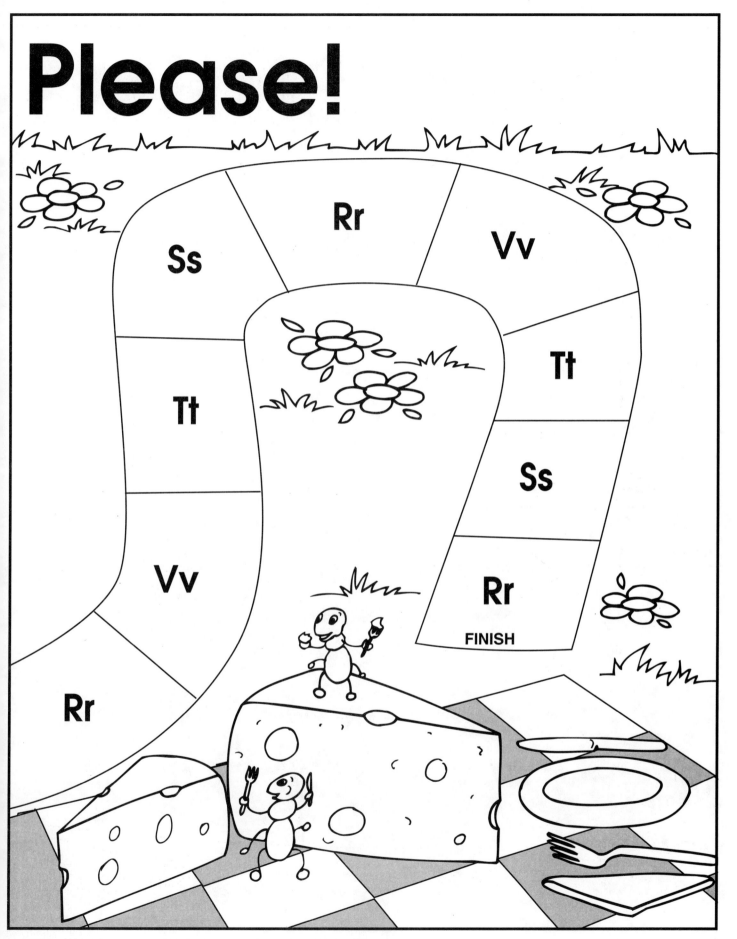

Center Pieces for "More Cheese Please!" Code the backs for self-checking.

Match each picture on page 163 to its matching initial consonant. Code the backs of the center pieces for self-checking if desired.

Going Ape

©The Education Center, Inc. • TEC874

Over Cookies

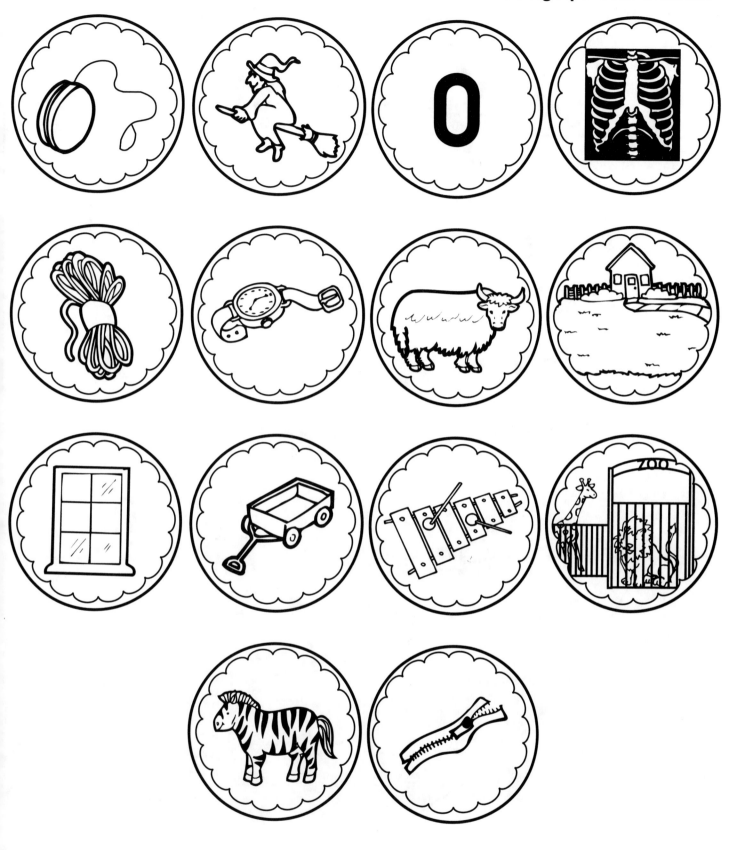

Note To Teacher: There are only two cookies for the Xx cookie jar.

Match each picture on page 167 to its matching initial consonant. Code the backs of the center pieces for self-checking if desired.

A Sweet

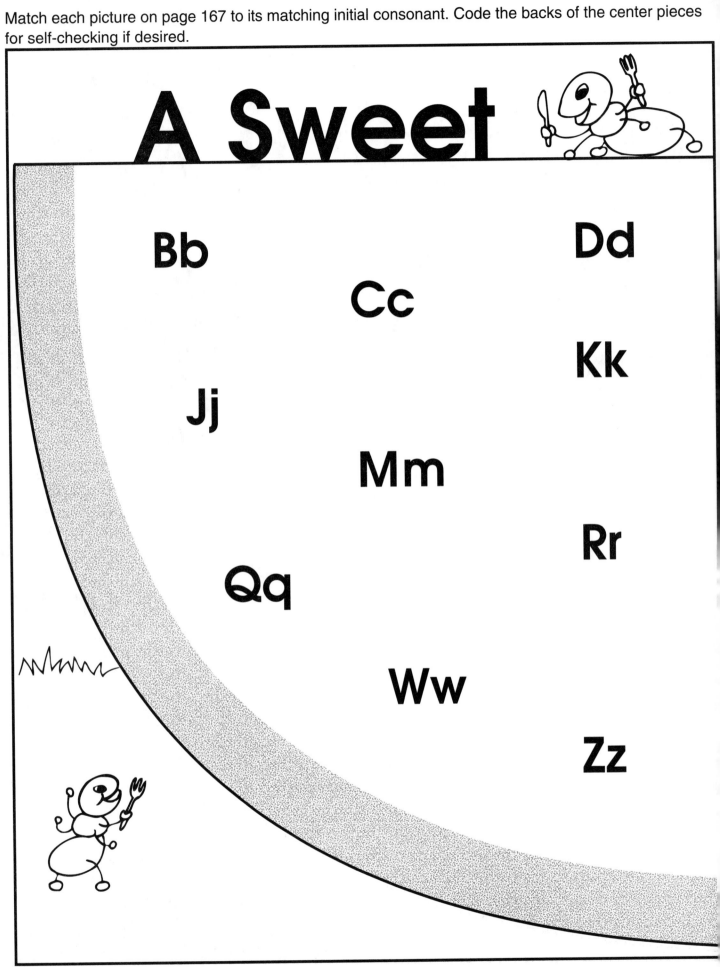

Bb

Dd

Cc

Kk

Jj

Mm

Rr

Qq

Ww

Zz

Slice...

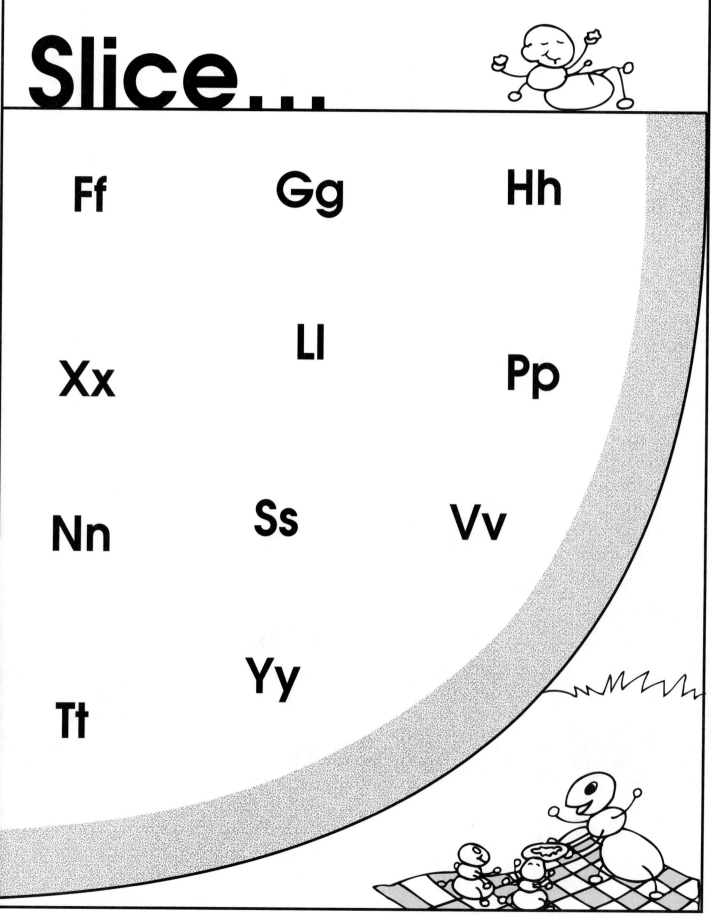

Ff   Gg   Hh

Ll

Xx   Pp

Nn   Ss   Vv

Yy

Tt

Student Evaluations And Awards

Use the worksheets in this section as an extended activity to review a unit or as an evaluation. "Apples," "Hippos," and "Clowns" are the three theme units presented to review and evaluate your students' progress. For a class activity, you may want to call out the word represented by each picture as your students follow along, coloring by the indicated sounds. Place duplicated sheets in an individualized learning center, or laminate your original and provide wipe-off crayons in various colors. These sheets will also make good take-home projects to involve parents in sound reinforcement.

A reproducible award follows each theme unit to recognize your students' progress and mastery of the initial consonant sounds.

Choice Pieces

Say the words. Listen for the beginning sound.

Color: l = red   p = brown
m = green
n = yellow

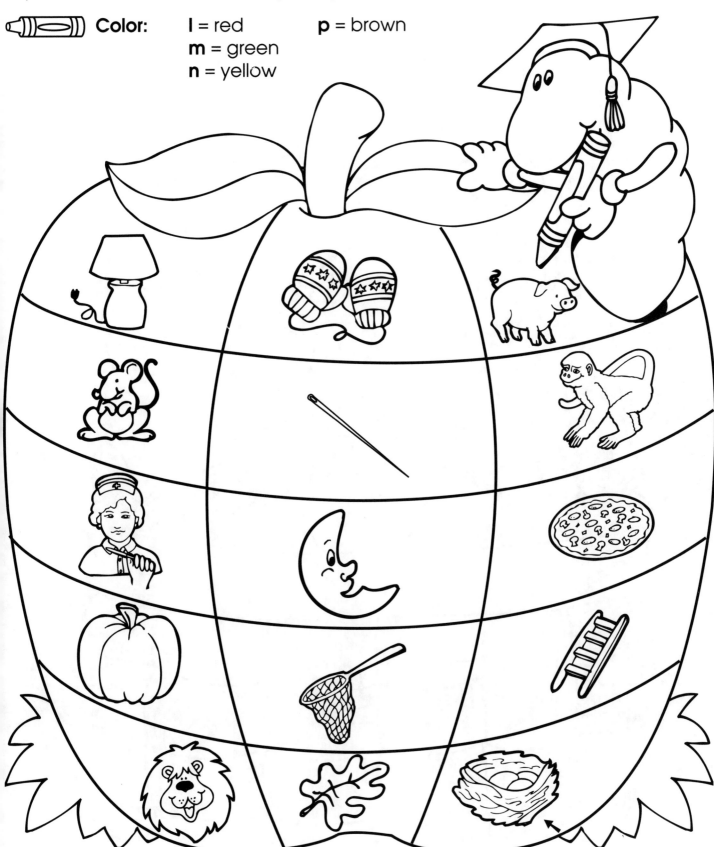

Name _____

A Snack To Munch

Say the words. Listen for the beginning sound.

Color: **b** = brown
f = yellow
g = green
k = red

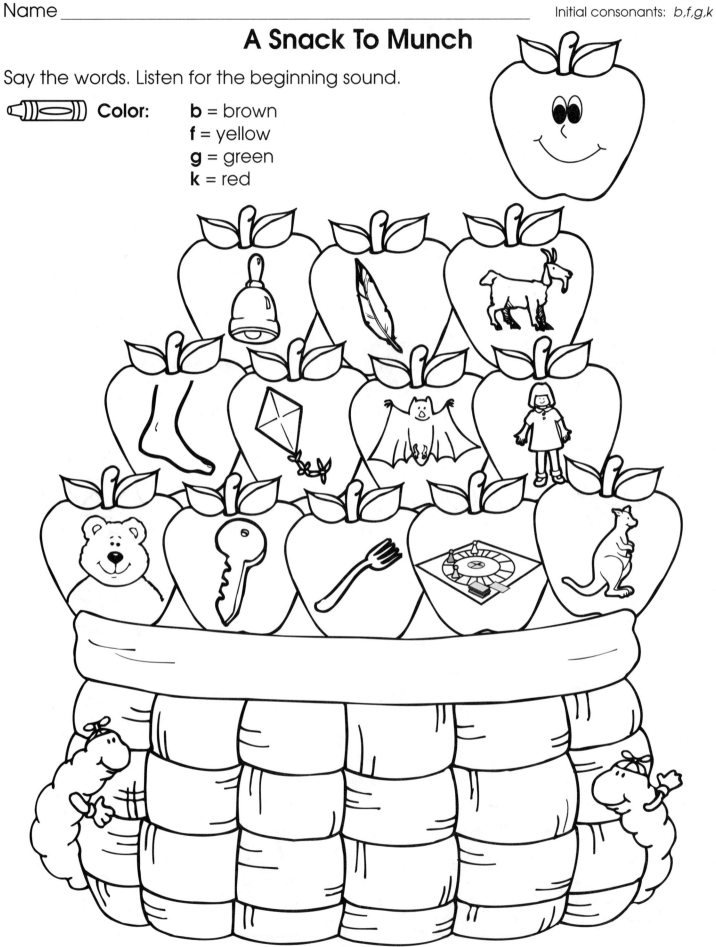

Name _____

Crunch And Munch

Say the words. Listen for the beginning sound.

Color: **v** = red
w = yellow
d = green

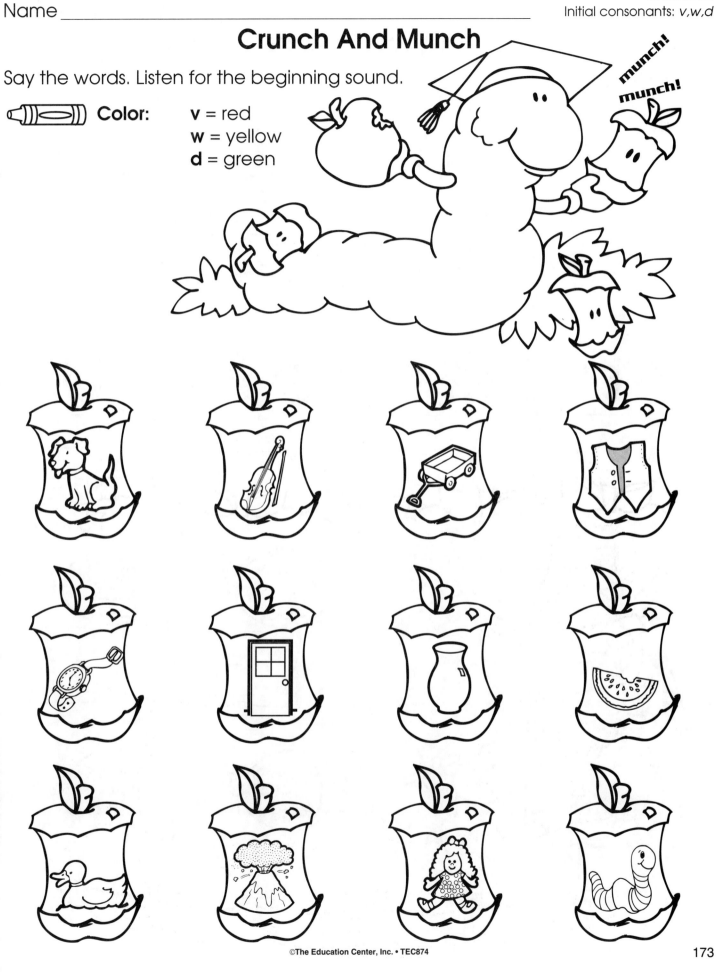

Name _____

Apple Friends

 Write the beginning letters.

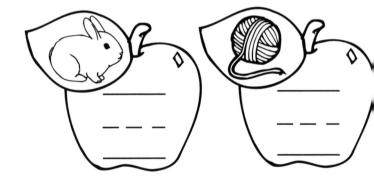

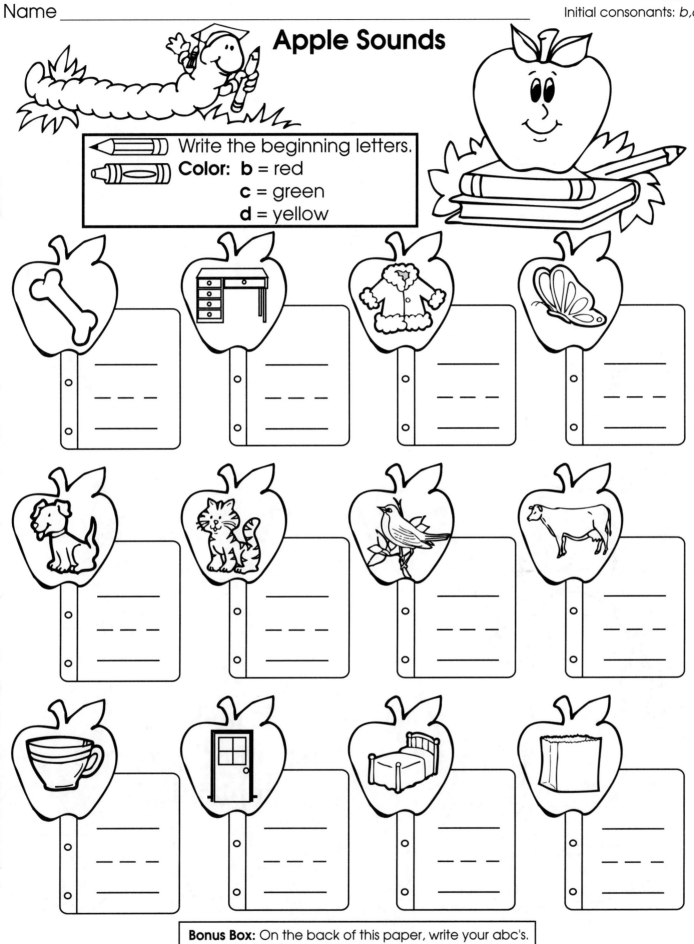

Name _____

Apple Sounds

Write the beginning letters.
Color: b = red
c = green
d = yellow

Bonus Box: On the back of this paper, write your abc's.

Extension Activities
Apples

— Upon completion of the unit, duplicate the reward below for recognition of "delicious" progress in phonics!

— Mask the words on the reward below and duplicate it to be used for center task cards for review and drill of consonant sounds.

— Duplicate the apple pattern on this page on red construction paper. Cut each apple in half and place a consonant picture on one half with the corresponding letter on the other half for the children to match.

Apple Pattern

Apple Reward

Name

is making "delicious" progress in phonics!

Name _____

Helping Hippos

Name each picture.
Color by the code.

Color Code

Hh—		red
Mm—		blue
Bb—		green
Ss—		yellow
Cc—		orange

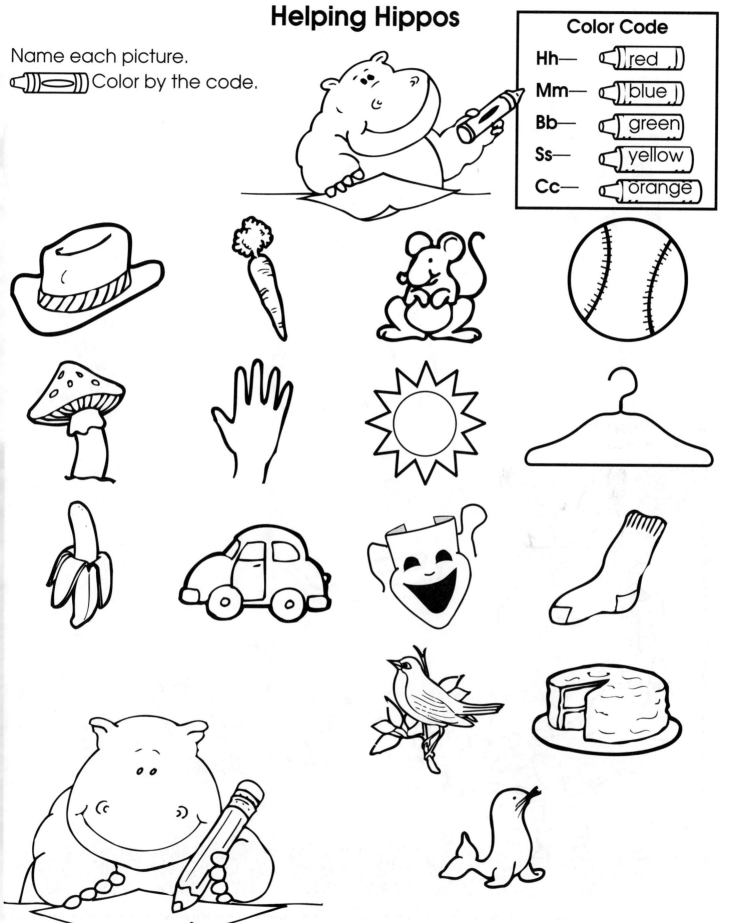

Cooking Up Beginning Sounds

Name each picture.

Color by the code.

Color Code		
Kk—red	**Ss**—green	**Tt**—orange
Jj—blue	**Yy**—yellow	

Name _____

©The Education Center, Inc. • TEC874

Name _____

Underwater Fun

Name each picture.

Color by the code.

Color Code		
Dd—orange	**Gg**—green	**Ll**—blue
Ff—purple	**Vv**—red	

Name _____

Cool Hippo!

Name each picture.

Circle the letter for the beginning sound.

Color.

Name _____

Delightful Dancers

Name each picture.

Color by the code.

Color Code		
Pp—red	**Nn**—yellow	**Ww**—orange
Qq—blue	**Rr**—green	

Follow-Up Activity

Use the hippo pattern below to create beginning sound flash cards for extra work on beginning sounds. You may decide to enlarge and duplicate the beginning sound pictures from the worksheets in this unit to put on your flash cards.

Pattern

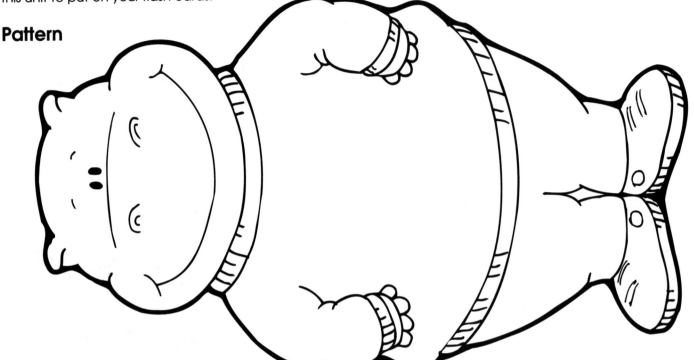

Reward—Send the reward below home to recognize progress in beginning sounds.

Hip, Hip, Hooray!

HOORAY!

_____
name

knows beginning sounds!

_____
teacher

_____
date

©The Education Center, Inc. • TEC874

Name _____

Flying High!

Look at the ◯.
Color the pictures that begin with that letter.

Name _____

Under The Big Top

Look at the picture.

 Write the beginning letter sound.

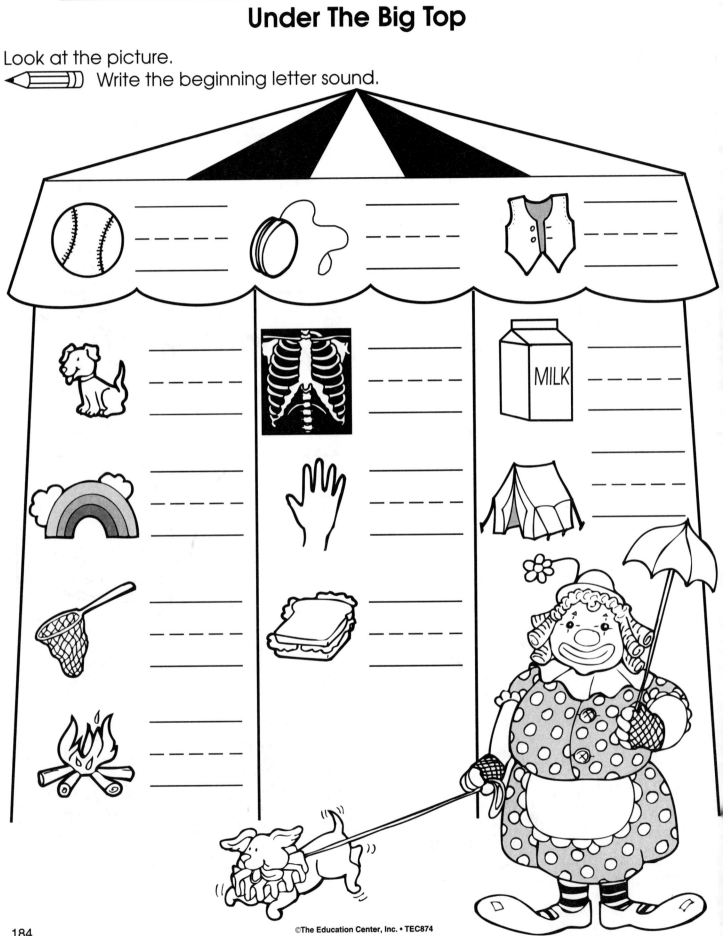

Cloudy-Day Clown

Name each picture.
Listen for the beginning sound.

 Color by the code:

Ll yellow   **Pp** green   **Ww** red   **Zz** blue

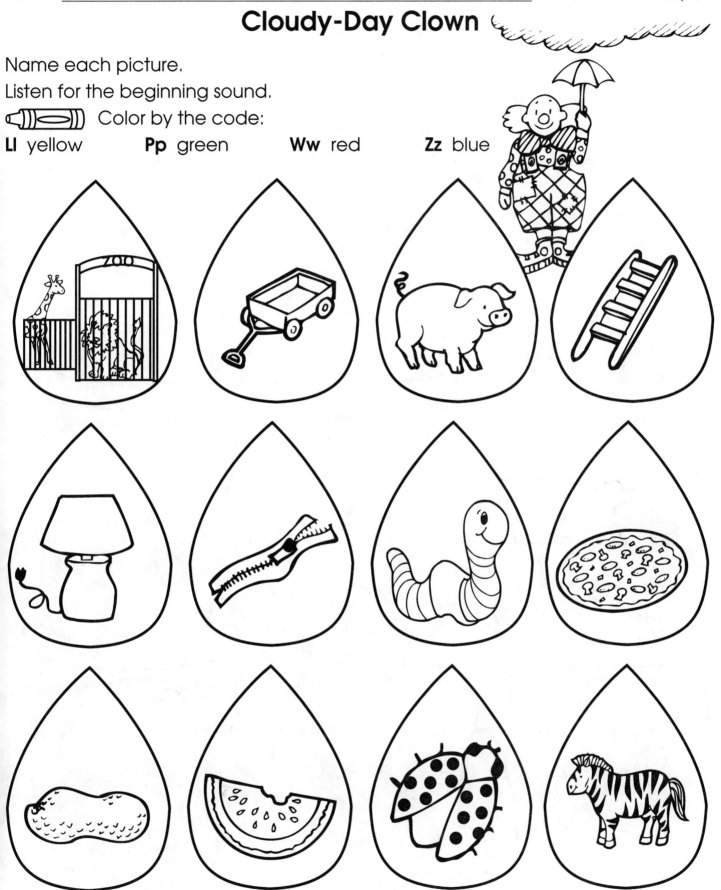

A Hat For Clown

Name each picture.

Circle the letter for the beginning sound.

Color.

Lighthearted Handful

Pattern

Follow-Up Activity
Use the clown pattern below to create beginning sound flash cards for extra work on beginning sounds. You may decide to enlarge and duplicate the beginning sound pictures from the worksheets in this unit to put on your flash cards.

Reward—Send the reward below home to recognize progress in beginning sounds.

_____ **is not**
student

Clowning Around
when it comes to
beginning sounds!

_____
teacher

_____
date

Bb

Cc

Dd

Ff

Gg

Hh

Jj

Kk

Ll

Note To Teacher: Duplicate these cards on construction paper for your classroom use.

Mm

Nn

Pp

Qq

Rr

Ss

Tt

Vv

Ww

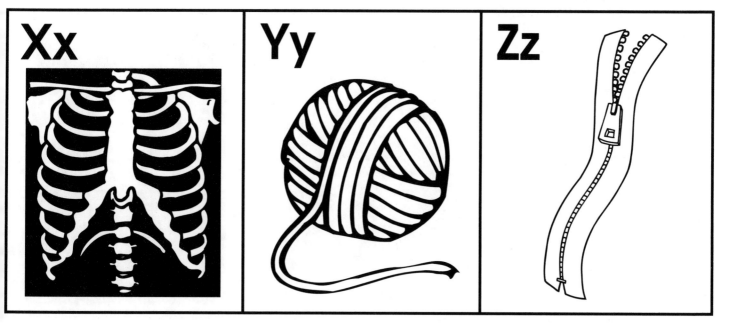

Xx

Yy

Zz